fresh

*… how new things come
to fresh hearts*

fresh

… how new things come

to fresh hearts

By Jim Hennesy

contents

foreword

The great author and thinker A.W. Tozer once said, *"What comes into our minds when we think about is the most important thing about us."*

In other words, our concept of will ultimately shape the construct of our life. So in an age where some would say the Church is irrelevant and the flames of vibrant Christianity have become dormant, Pastor Jim Hennesy has written a book that will reignite the flickering embers of even the most fragile faith. FRESH reminds us that the thing that should come to our minds when we think about is His desire and profound ability to bring about the NEW.

I've had the incredible privilege over the last 25 years to not only sit under Pastor Jim's leadership, but to look into his life, and what I've learned has been invaluable. My grandmother use to say, "Honey, I would rather see a sermon than hear a sermon any day." When I was seven years old I had absolutely no clue what my grandmother meant, but time has unlocked its meaning. I now understand that the decibel of our lives should speak just as loud, if not louder, than any of the sermons we preach. In essence, true impact is never really made in fleeting moments of intensity but rather in faithful years of consistency.

There is a myriad of words I could use to define Jim Hennesy: LEADER, FATHER, HUSBAND, WISE, LOYAL, FIGHTER, and FRIEND. However, if I could borrow from the brilliant mind of Tozer, the first thing that comes to mind when I think of Jim Hennesy is CONSISTENCY. Perhaps the paradox of a spirit-infused, -pleasing, FRESH life is that it must first begin with a quiet commitment to be consistent.

It is Pastor Jim's unwavering commitment to life and ministry that makes this book not only riveting, but necessary for the 21st century church. As you read each page, it is my earnest prayer that your life be infused with a transcendent hope, that can only come from an unchanging who is the same yesterday, today, forever and yet still declares: BEHOLD! I DO A NEW THING!

—*Robert Madu*
Robert Madu Ministries

dedication

This book is dedicated to the man who
taught me Jesus. His words and deeds
revealed a Loving Father.
See you in heaven, Dad.

I will give you the keys of the Kingdom

of heaven; whatever you bind on earth

will be bound in heaven, and whatever you loose

on earth will be loosed in heaven.

Matthew 16:19

CHAPTER 1

How to Live *fresh*

FRESH: not previously known or used; new or different. (*Webster's Dictionary*)

And now we are brothers and sisters in GOD's *family because of the blood of Jesus, and he welcomes us to come into the most holy sanctuary in the heavenly realm—boldly and without hesitation. For he has dedicated a NEW, life-giving way for us to approach* GOD...*to give us free and FRESH access to him...*
Hebrews 10:35

fresh access to Him...

One of my favorite authors, Malcolm Gladwell, wrote in his book, "The Tipping Point" how little things make a big difference. He describes a moment of critical mass, the threshold, where one additional snowflake creates an avalanche causing an entire mountain to rush in a new direction...when one additional cell gets infected with a virus, and turns to cancer...when one guy's idea about selling shoes turns into providing shoes for whole villages in Africa.

1

One of my life tipping points occurred when I met Becky, now my wife of 41 years, in college. We spent time together. We liked each other. After many conversations together, sharing our hopes and dreams, one conversation turned into two, and one rainy night in Smith Park, our lives began rushing together in a new direction—we wanted to spend the rest of our lives together. Once we reached that pinnacle, our conversations were different—more focused, intimate, long-term. It was new. It was exciting. And it was refreshing! A whole new world opened before us!

Can you recall a tipping point that changed the trajectory of your life?

There was a time in Jesus' ministry when he explained how the Kingdom worked. He instructed us to never put new wine into old wineskins. (Matthew 9:17) Why was that such a problem? In that day, when travelling with filled wineskins, the sediment and heat caused the old wineskin to become dry, even dirty. It reached a tipping point and became stretched and brittle as the wine fermented inside. If new wine was poured into the old wineskin it burst, making both the wine and the wineskin useless.

But when a new wineskin was used for storage, it allowed flexibility for the new wine to settle, be secured, stay fresh and be available to drink. Jesus' admonition is not referring to old vs. young. Age actually has nothing to do with it. It's not pitting tradition against contemporary. It's not even juxtaposing Old Testament vs. New Testament. The point: fresh is better than stale.

Can you recall the aroma of fresh Krispy Kreme donuts when the "light is on" announcing to all the optimum time to buy one? Can you conjure in your mind the smell of the morning dew? Fresh flowers just picked? Or a carrot pulled from the garden, washed with a hose, and that crunching first bite? That's what this parable is about...the novel...the undiscovered. The NEW.

We are a new creation and all things have become new.
2 Corinthians 5:17

We are PROMISED a freshness of God to be poured upon each generation. We are guaranteed that the freshness of God will permeate future generations, and, to an even greater degree than we have seen in our lifetime. Future generations will discover more beauty, new power, new splendor, more glory of God. The future demands the new.

If you are a seasoned believer, you may have the tendency to think you have discovered most, if not all, there is to know of faith, goodness, power, or wisdom. But if you just let yourself go back in time and remember life without a cell phone, without Google, without Twitter, you will realize, with all of those options for information currently available, society will keep improving, continue inventing, discovering, and surpassing what we know now.

The same applies to God and his Word. At least, that is what the scripture promises:

...for there is no end to the discovery of the greatness that
surrounds you. Generation after generation will declare
more of your greatness and more of your glory.
Psalm 145:4

Only *fresh* Can Contain New

Here was the problem for the Jewish people. Something new appeared—Jesus—and caused uproar in their culture.

Jesus caused life to rush in a different direction. Incrementally, throughout the ages, promises (promises made throughout the Old Testament) gained traction and momentum until finally Jesus burst onto the scene bringing another option—a new, FRESH way.

Instead of slaughtering and burning a sacrifice for sins, Jesus said, "I am the way, the truth, and the life. No man comes to the Father, but through me."
John 14:6

This one concept alone completely radicalized the Jewish culture. All they had known was God in the rock, God in the bush, God in the wind...now here was God in the FLESH! Here came a revelation suggesting they were a generation who would experience something new...something radical...something holy...something FRESH!

Of course, the issue was not "what happened" but their reaction to what happened! Their minds were not prepared for it. Their greatest obstacle to accepting God's beautiful plan of sending his Son to earth for our sins was their own mindset! The greatest power on earth is your attitude (mindset). Sometimes attitude seems stronger than God!

You see, the children of Israel witnessed the opening of the Red Sea. They had been delivered from the plagues in Egypt. They had eaten the food provided from heaven each and every day. But when it came to "something new," AKA the Promised Land...they sent 12 spies to make the decision for the whole group! The majority of those spies (10) reported that it was just too risky to go to a new place—the unknown, the unexpected, the GIANTS!

Each time God decides to bring you into a new place with Him, YOU are the one who decides if you will go. **Even God himself does not have the power to make you do what your mind refuses to do!**

What if Joshua had decided NOT to march around those walls? What if David had decided to hide in the cave with his brothers? What if Noah had determined building an ark was simply too hard? And what about Mary and Joseph's unexplainable pregnancy? Too hard. Too risky. Too crazy. Too unreasonable. Too unbelievable.

The greatest battles and life-changing events are not what actually take place externally in your city, your church or your family. The greatest battle takes place in your MIND.

In fact, that bunch of Hebrews in the wilderness were on the edge of forfeiting the "new," the FRESH, simply on a report from 10 people! Actually, they DID postpone entering the land they were promised...for 40 years!

Don't let YOUR mind be the obstacle for missing the FRESH God wants for you, your business, and your family. Be ready and willing to be that person who opens wide for FRESH!

The Question

One day Jesus gathered his best and his brightest and asked one of those riveting questions:

"Who do you say that I am?"
Matthew 16:13

This question was on the heels of offering the key to defeat evil, liberate millions held in slavery, despair, shame, and psychological breakdown. This question was a "set up" to announce a NEW and FRESH way of living!

When you visit Israel, you can visit Caesarea Philippi, the place where this question and ensuing conversation occurred. In this case, the geography is important. Caesarea lies on the Mediterranean coast. It boasts a Roman amphitheater and the historic Herodean port. There is also an archaeological dig with pillars, sculptures, the remains of frescoes and a mosaic floor. The Jewish people recognized it as the headquarters for Baal, a location of child sacrifice, and a center for demonic rituals.

For the Greeks, Caesarea Philippi was the birthplace of Pan (a pagan god that was half human, with the legs and the horns of a goat), who represented sexual favors and seduction. For the Romans, this was a place where Caesar worshipped and declared his deity. For centuries, political power, wealth, and war reigned in this region.

So now you see the backdrop of where Jesus had travelled, and where he decided to ask such a loaded question: *"Who do you say that I am?"*

This conversation did not occur in Galilee, where he had fed thousands of men, women and children on the hillside. He wasn't at Lazarus' house, where he raised Lazarus from the dead. Jesus didn't ask the question in the temple, synagogue or on the ruins of Jericho where great walls came tumbling down. He took his men to a sterile desert, a pagan seat of power—a hard place—and asked them against the backdrop of pagan gods and sexual perversion.

At this time in his ministry—in this awkward, pagan setting—the 12 men who had observed, heard, and learned from him over many months were stunned when Jesus called their bluff. He asked them to focus and answer out loud...*What do you think of me? What are you willing to SAY about me here?* When you are encompassed with bad news; when the boss is harassing you, your children are ignoring you, cancer spreads or loneliness has consumed you, Jesus will ask you the same question: "Who do you think that I am? What are you willing to say about me now?"

We need a FRESH answer! Not one that your mother told you. Not one your grandmother spoke about. Not one you memorized ten years ago, when you first became a believer in Jesus. You need a FRESH answer; an answer built on FRESH revelation; on a FRESH word from God. One that has been poured into your heart from scripture, through a test or a timely word from a friend. You need NEW insight to the old God of grace.

The Answer

So now...in this setting...in this circumstance...at this time of Jesus' ministry...Peter brilliantly answered:

"You are the Messiah, the Son of the living God!"

Jesus erupts! "Peter! That's perfect! You get it! And because you know who I am, you know yourself! Your identity and emotions are established on this revelation."

I will give you the keys of the Kingdom of heaven; whatever
you bind on earth will be bound in heaven, and whatever
you loose on earth will be loosed in heaven.
Matthew 16:19

This is new POWER! This is FRESH revelation. This is a life-changing mindset! **Because I know who the Messiah is... therefore, I know how I can go forward with success!**

Notice Peter's answer was based on revelation—not rationale. Whatever hell you are facing, once you discover a FRESH revelation in that circumstance, in specific chaos, in fearful insecurity...once you know He is the Christ, the all-powerful, all-knowing, all-encompassing I AM, then you can FRESHLY declare without equivocation, whatever hell you face will never prevail!

This is the rock on which I will put together my church,
a church so expansive with energy that not even
the gates of hell will be able to keep it out.
Matthew 16:18, The Message

Peter's faith is impressive here, but Jesus' faith was the tipping point. Jesus did not say, "I will prevail against the gates of hell." He said that my church, believers together, will be such an overpowering force the gates of hell won't be able to thwart that power!

I've visited the gates of Caesarea Philippi, where this conversation took place. I wish I could adequately paint you the picture. The "gates of hell" were actually referring to caves carved out at the bottom of a cliff, where detestable and hedonistic acts of worship to false gods took place. Water flowed from this cliff, and the common belief at the time was that gods travelled to and from the underworld through those caves. Truly, Caesarea Philippi was the "gates of hell."

The power of the Gates represents demonic, hellish, pagan, cultural hedonism prevalent in society. And even today, those forces are real and out to destroy you. But Jesus' words declare **those gates will not prevail against you.**

You may be facing an overwhelming obstacle, a lawsuit, someone has schemed to steal, kill, or destroy you, your family or your business. It's hot here in Texas, where I live, but hell is not hot enough, strong enough or clever enough to prevail in your life or in your family.

There is a significant gap between what the church is today and what it could be. Yet, as long as there is a body of believers under construction here on earth, the gates of hell cannot prevail.

It's not a secret that the church is messy. The church is frustrating, dumb, embarrassing, neglectful...because the church consists of people. And people are messy, frustrating, dumb, embarrassing, neglectful...you get the point. So that wineskin is brittle...stiff...inflexible. It's not always ready to receive the FRESH.

A number of years ago, my mom and dad retired from serving a Christian university. They served there 18 years and gave it their best. When a new president arrived, a national magazine wrote an article blasting the former administration (my dad) and reported his leadership in a bad light. My wife, Becky, was furious! She wrote a letter to the board of directors, calling them to task for the inaccurate portrayal of my dad's tenure there. You see, what she read in the magazine versus what she knew to be true were completely contradictory. All of us were hurt by the behavior of the church.

If you've been hurt, disappointed or disillusioned by the church, friends, family—well, frankly, anybody (and we all have)—it is difficult to stay FRESH, supple and ready to receive the NEW that God has for us.

But, here's the secret to remaining FRESH!

PREVAIL

Webster's dictionary defines prevail as "to prove to be stronger; to prove to be effective; to predominate; to be current." But I love the definition from scripture:

*So now we must cling tightly to the hope that lives within us,
knowing that Goᴅ always keeps his promises.*
Hebrews 10:23

It's the promise the enemy tries to mutilate. The enemy puts fear, doubt and frustration in our mind so we will forget who God is and forget who we are in God. Evil is nothing new to us. Hell always assaults, schemes, competes...because hell knows that if/when we start receiving NEW (new values, new revelation, new dreams), the devil doesn't stand a chance of winning.

Do you know the story of Jezebel? She was sneaky, seductive, and religious...in short, a dream killer. She killed a guy for his garden! She harassed worshippers. Then God brought someone NEW to the scene—Elijah! Elijah became a prevailing bearer of Good News—for miracles, victories, rain...and that nation turned! Jezebel fell out of a window to her death, her body ravaged by dogs, and her carcass was like *"dung on the ground." (II Kings 9:13)* Quite a poor ending to her life.

I'm sure you've heard of Goliath. He was more than a giant. He was hell's effort to stop God's purpose. God built in David something NEW. David had a mindset that he could, in fact, kill Goliath. As he prevailed, his entire nation turned in a new direction!

What about Herod, part of the Christmas story? He wanted so desperately to hold on to his power that he killed all the babies he could find. But God chose Mary, sent wise men, placed stars in the sky, and gave men dreams—something NEW, each one—to protect his plan of sending his Son to earth—God's grace and plan prevailed.

Don't forget Nebuchadnezzar. For a while, King Nebuchadnezzar had the upper hand. He legislated a secular worship system for all to follow. But three young men refused. They experienced the power of something new and FRESH— God's presence with them in the fire—and were delivered out of that fire, unharmed! Shadrach, Meshach, and Abednego were thrown into the furnace—yet prevailed.

History is filled with ancient evidence! God's people prevailed over Jezebel, Goliath, Herod, Pharaoh, Haman, Judas, Pilate, the sons of Sceva, the Athenians, Hitler, Jim Crowe, poverty, addictions, and cancer! And God wants you to have NEW stories, NEW dreams, FRESH testimonies and PREVAIL! Whatever is against you is not greater than the ONE who is building you—FRESH and new!

You are not a victim of the gates of hell. You are the LIGHT OF THE WORLD! You are a prevailing force! Read the Word of God. Talk about your faith. Put your faith into action every day—something as simple as a smile or a nice big tip to your server. Or volunteer in your community or church. Whatever it takes to stay FRESH so God can unveil NEW!

As you stay fresh about who Jesus is in your life, and stay fresh about who you are in God, you will attain the new wineskin to receive every FRESH gift he offers for your generation, and for those generations to come who will remember and recount the blessings of God from your life.

PREVAIL Together

Once you have embraced the authority of prevailing, be attuned to creative ways to encourage, show compassion, build up and motivate others toward the FRESH God has for them. John Maxwell, best-selling author, says everyone is looking for attention and affirmation. This sounds like an invitation to bring the hurting around you words of comfort and blessings of peace!

Prevailing together involves leaning in, not pulling away or neglecting others. Being there. Listening. Caring. It's these simple daily acts that not only strengthen others, but will strengthen you.

The word "homothumadon" is a Greek word translated "together." It is context for a lot of the action recorded in the Book of Acts:

...apostles performed many miraculous signs and wonders among the people and all believers used to meet together (homothumadon) on Solomon's Porch. More and more men and women believed in the LORD and were added to their number.
Acts 5:12, 13

All believers were of one heart and one mind (homothumadon) and with great power they gave witness to the resurrection of Jesus...
Acts 4:32

Can you see that the secret of the early church was not doctrine, not talents, not methods, not sinlessness? It was togetherness! Same fire! Same passion! The same FRESHNESS, prevailing together!

FRESH is the opposite of stagnant. Is it time for you to dream again? Your destiny is not a finish line that God draws in the sand. Destiny is developed, dreamed about, and fulfilled with new and FRESH revelation!

✔ fresh Checkup:

1. Does your faith feel "OLD"? Can you identify new dimensions of grace or reasons for praise?

2. Can you recall a time when someone energized your spirit? What did they do specifically?

3. What else refreshes your spirit?

When you come looking for me,

you'll find me. Yes, when you get

serious about finding me

and want it more than anything else,

I'll make sure you won't be disappointed.

I'll turn things around for you.

Jeremiah 29:13

CHAPTER 2

*fr*esh Strength

STRENGTH: power, force, energy, the ability to exert
effort; may imply latent or exerted physical, mental,
or spiritual ability to act or be acted upon.
(Webster's Dictionary)

David strengthened himself with trust in his GOD.
1 Samuel 30:6

*Haven't I commanded you? Strength! Courage! Don't
be timid; don't get discouraged. GOD, your GOD,
is with you every step you take.*
Joshua 1:9

Recently I took a road trip to Houston. I made a pit stop, and while filling up with gas, a good 'ole Texas cowboy (he was wearing a cowboy hat!) approached me. He looked at my truck and began asking me all about it: did it have a back-up camera, leather seats, and automatic warnings if it drifted out of the lane, and 4-wheel drive? Finally, after answering all his intrusive questions, I responded, "Why do you want to know?" His answer was simple, "I just don't want to pay for a bunch of stuff I won't ever use." I replied, "I'm not sure you NEED all that stuff, but when you're climbing thru the mountains, and the mud is flying—there's nothing like it! I like the extra stuff and I use it!"

Did Jesus pay for things on the cross that we will never use?

The word "strength" (Hebrew—chazaq) is the same in both verses above and is used over 300 times in the Bible. Its primitive root meaning is to fasten upon; to seize, be strong, courageous, cure, help, repair, fortify; to bind, restrain, conquer; catch, cleave, confirm, be constant, constrain, continue, be of good (take) courage, be sure, take hold, be urgent, behave valiantly, withstand. Well, I think you get the idea!

And why did God command Joshua and David to become strong? Because their situation demanded strength! The strength of God is always connected to a specific opportunity. Did God need Joshua to lead the march around the walls of a city? Did God need David to slay the giant, Goliath? For sure, God gave those guys strength because he had a specific task in mind for them. He had a purpose, a destiny, a calling which only they could accomplish—not in their own strength, but in the strength He provided.

What is your opportunity that requires fresh strength? Are you broadcasting His marvelous wonders? That's your opportunity. Are you representing God to people you meet? That's your JOB. And people should do their job. If the president is playing golf while North Korea is testing warheads...if the bank is being robbed while police are at the donut shop...if there is a trauma victim in the emergency room but the doctor is flirting with a nurse...that's not what should happen. The world works better when people do their jobs!

And that is exactly the reason you need fresh strength—to handle the task for which you were destined. It's time for you to seize your opportunity and see it accomplished. And that requires *fresh strength*.

But you are GOD's chosen treasure—priests who are kings, a spiritual "nation" set apart as GOD's devoted ones. He called you out of darkness to experience his marvelous light, and now he claims you as his very own. He did this so that you would broadcast his glorious wonders throughout the world.
I Peter 2:9-10

Jesus talks about His Kingdom throughout the New Testament. He compares it to wineskins, explains it to His disciples, and tells them they are going to be able to do even greater things than He did once He sends His spirit to dwell in them and enable them.

But they needed to be ready. They would require fresh strength. It would be necessary to discard their entrenched ideas and develop a new mindset in order to embrace their assignments. The greatest hindrance to God's plan for your life is not the devil or generational curses. Your greatest hindrance is your own mindset.

The Bible is filled with stories of expanding mindsets which produce fresh strength. God is good, yet God is powerful, too. God was in the temple but now He is resurrection and the Light, and the soon-coming King. We were servants of God but now he calls us friends. Jesus was a carpenter, yet He has all authority in heaven and earth. You see, every page of the Bible brings a new discovery!

Abraham discovered old people can have babies. Jonah survived three days in a whale's belly and discovered enemies can convert. Meshach, Shadrach, and Abednego discovered fire doesn't consume you when God is with you in the furnace. David discovered the power of a sling. Ezekiel discovered dead bones can be resurrected, reconnected and become an army. The disciples discovered Jesus could multiply food, quiet storms, and rise from the dead. Peter discovered that God loves Gentiles. Paul discovered God loves murderers.

What will you discover about God? About yourself? About His plan for you? You can discover FRESH STRENGTH—strength for the task, and strength for your journey. But it comes from expanding your perceptions and faith.

You have fought the addiction for a dozen years. Is there any hope of freedom?

You've suffered four miscarriages. Where is God's goodness?

You've dreamed of marriage and a family, but you are 35, single, and tired. Where is God?

Often God's people struggle to keep their enthusiasm. Not evil. Just exhausted! Long-term disappointments can only be defeated by fresh strength.

Most of us know we need a change of mindset. We must pay more attention to how we see things so we can adjust our view to see the way God views it, and live in harmony with the mind of Christ. Since the old mindset usually seems stronger than the new one, we need a fresh outpouring of strength in order to embrace the fresh mindset of discovery just waiting for us.

Philip told his friend, Nathanael that he met Jesus from Nazareth. Nathanael's response was predictable:

Nathanael sneered, "Nazareth! What good thing could ever come from Nazareth?" Philip answered, "Come and let's find out!" When Jesus saw Nathanael approaching, he said, "Now here comes a true son of Israel—an honest man with no hidden motive!"

Nathanael was stunned and said, "But you've never met me—how do you know anything about me?" Jesus answered, "Nathanael, right before Philip came to you I saw you sitting under the shade of a fig tree."

Nathanael blurted out, "Teacher, you are truly the Son of God and the King of Israel!"

Jesus answered, "Do you believe simply because I told you I saw you sitting under a fig tree? You will experience even more impressive things than that!"
John 1:46-50

Nathanael discovered something new which caused him to believe Jesus was the Son of God! His mind was changed. Good things can come from Nazareth! As a result of a changed perspective, Nathaniel began a new life.

In I Samuel 30 there is an obscure story regarding David.

David had already been selected to be the king, but his internship was anything but easy. He is dodging spears thrown by a crazy man. There was a bounty on his head. David was trying to be and do good, but he found himself in the wilderness.

Mindsets are mostly formed
in the wilderness

Wilderness brings out the best and the worst in people. And it is a great place to meet God. While David was in the wilderness he attracted wilderness people. Not professionals. Not socialites. Not the powerful. He gathered misfits and social outcasts.

Soon David grew weary, lost, and overwhelmed with running. He was disappointed with people. He was tired of eating wilderness food. He ended up taking 600 soldiers into mercenary employment against Israel's enemy, the Philistine leader, King Achish. At this point, he was actually living among the enemy, and double-crossing them. He even pretended to attack his own people and actually looted from other enemies and delivered it to the Philistines. What a sneaky guy! Not a pretty picture for a future king. But read ahead...

Three days later, David and his men arrived back in Ziklag [their current home]...By the time David and his men entered the village, it had been burned to the ground, and their wives, sons, and daughters all taken prisoner.

David and his men burst out in loud wails—wept and wept until they were exhausted with weeping. David's two wives...had been taken prisoner along with the rest. And suddenly David was in even worse trouble. There was talk among the men, bitter over the loss of their families, of stoning him.

David strengthened himself with trust in his GOD. He ordered Abiathar the priest, "Bring me the ephod so I can consult GOD." Abiathar brought it to David.

In the midst of the smoldering rubble of Ziklag, his camp-site, David prayed, worshipped, and called on his pastor, Abiathar. Together they looked at the ephod. Now the ephod was something like an apron, with attached stones of the Urim and Thumin (part of the breastplate of the priest). David was wearing an ephod when he danced in the streets before the Lord. And it was also considered useful when needing insightful counsel or prophetic proclamations from God. The ephod gave God's guidance, and if anyone ever needed guidance, it was David. His world seemed to be collapsing.

So David turned to God.

Then David prayed to GOD, "Shall I go after these raiders? Can I catch them?"

The answer came, "Go after them! Yes, you'll catch them! Yes, you'll make the rescue!"

After receiving direction, he and 600 of his men began the journey. After 15 miles to the brook, 200 of the men were so exhausted they couldn't keep going. No strength. No spirit. No song. Maybe you've been at that point in your life. Exhausted faith. Lost hope. No more joy. You've lost your dream. You have journeyed as far as you can go.

But 400 remaining soldiers crossed over the Brook Besor and pushed deeper to find the guys who had raided their territory. Then the story takes a turn—a tipping point.

The soldiers meet a sick Egyptian. Instead of ignoring him and kicking him aside, David gave him food and water and saved his life! David knew what it was like to be in the desert and sick.

GOD's love is meteoric,
his loyalty astronomic,
His purpose titanic,
his verdicts oceanic.
Yet in his largeness
nothing gets lost;
Not a man, not a mouse,
slips through the cracks.
How exquisite your love, O GOD!
How eager we are to run under your wings,
To eat our fill at the banquet you spread
as you fill our tankards with Eden spring water.
You're a fountain of cascading light,
and you open our eyes to light.
Keep on loving your friends;
do your work in welcoming hearts.
Don't let the bullies kick me around,
the moral midgets slap me down.
Send the upstarts sprawling
flat on their faces in the mud.
Psalms 36:5-12, The Message

David remembered what God had done for him, and he passed it on to the sick Egyptian. And that is what God's people do! **We give what we have been given. And by giving we are strengthened.** David's care for the hurt guy turned his situation around!

David asked him [the Egyptian], "Can
you take us to the raiders?"

"Promise me by God," he said, "that you won't kill me or turn me over to my old master, and I'll take you straight to the raiders."

He led David to them. They were scattered all over the place, eating and drinking, gorging themselves on all the loot they had plundered from Philistia and Judah.

David pounced. He fought them from before sunrise until evening of the next day...David rescued everything the Amalekites had taken. And he rescued his two wives! Nothing and no one was missing. David recovered everything.

As you read above, the Egyptian gives David the location of the looters and makes them sitting ducks for David and his men. The recovery was fabulous! Everything lost is returned. A ridiculous triumph! David is liked and trusted again. They recovered ALL!

Of course, the best part was that once they had joined back up with the 200 left beside the brook, David had an opportunity to show real leadership. His 400 warriors bristled at the idea of sharing the spoils with those who had faltered along the way. But David intervened. In I Samuel 30: 23-25 he declared:

"Families don't do this sort of thing! Oh no, my brothers!" said David as he broke up the argument. "You can't act this way with what God gave us! God kept us safe. He handed over the raiders who attacked us. Who would ever listen to this kind of talk? The share of the one who stays with the gear is the share of the one who fights—equal shares. Share and share alike!" From that day on, David made that the rule in Israel—and it still is.

David understood that we must treat people with the grace we receive. If you hold on to the help God sends you, it stagnates. Strength becomes fresh when you share it.

The Lord Gives Strength

DAVID! "He STRENGTHENED himself in the Lord." (I Samuel 30:6)

This word, chazaq, is used here again. He found his FRESH STRENGTH in God. This fresh strength led him to discover a new and unused dimension of God.

F—Focus R—Recovery E—Energy S—Strength H—Hope

Paul states unequivocally, *"I can do all things through Christ who strengthens me."* (Philippians 4:13)

Jesus says, *"Come to me all who are weary and heavy-laden, and I will give you strength [refreshing]."* (Matthew 11:28)

David offers us a true-life story showing us real strength and guidance. God wants to provide strength for you in your present circumstance. God is not a concept. He is your Savior. Your healer. Your provider. He himself is clothed in strength. Through Him you can discover strength and a spirit-led strategy to tear down the strongholds in your life.

Strength comes from Seeking

So David inquired of the Lord, "Shall I pursue?" And GOD answered, "Pursue. For you shall surely overtake them and without fail recover all."
I Samuel 30:8

David did not bury himself in self-pity. He did not throw his hands in the air and give up.

Don't expect to live fresh and experience fresh strength if you are not willing to seek the Lord.

When you come looking for me, you'll find me. Yes, when you get serious about finding me and want it more than anything else, I'll make sure you won't be disappointed. I'll turn things around for you.
Jeremiah 29:13

Strength and Caring go Together

David's caring was communal. It was not just for the wives. Not just for the 400 men. Even the exhausted 200 men were extended grace.

But David went a step further. He sent thank-you gifts to other leaders:

On returning to Ziklag, David sent portions of the plunder to the elders of Judah, his neighbors, with a note saying, "A gift from the plunder of Goᴅ's enemies!" He sent them to the elders in Bethel, Ramoth Negev…and Hebron, along with several other places David and his men went to from time to time.
I Samuel 30:26-31

And his reputation spread far and wide! And in the next chapter of his life, Saul, the current king, disappears, and David begins his rule. The stage was set for David to have a successful reign as king.

What if the thing that is exhausting you today is the very thing that exalts you tomorrow? What if the circumstance that almost destroys you becomes an opportunity where you discover a new, FRESH aspect of God? A place where, when you are broken, you experience breakthrough! That's the definition of FRESH STRENGTH.

The KEY: GIVE what you have already received and you will receive more!

✔ strength Checkup:

1. Can you remember the last desperate time in your life? How did you survive?

2. Are you aware of someone needing God's help? What can you do to impart it?

GOD always makes his grace visible in Christ,

who includes us as partners of his endless triumph.

Through our yielded lives he spreads the

fragrance of the knowledge

of GOD everywhere we go.

II Corinthians 2:14

CHAPTER 3

fresh Oil

OIL: liquid substances from plant, animal, or mineral sources

---

The term *yitshar* (fresh oil) occurs twenty-one times in the Bible, and frequently referred to the fresh olive oil produce of the land, which was a sign of the Lord's blessing of prosperity, while the loss or lack of it was a sign of his judgment.

Olive trees took a long time to grow and mature, but they also lasted for hundreds of years. Therefore, a good oil supply was a sign of stability. Oil was used as a commodity of trade or personal income, for various kinds of common daily consumption—as part of the bread diet in tabernacle grain offerings, as fuel for lamps in the tabernacle, or homes, as a lubricant for one's hair and skin, sometimes used with a special sense of honor, as an aromatic substance, as a medication, or in healing contexts, for royal and religious ritual procedures. *(Baker's Evangelical Dictionary of Biblical Theology)*

Your anointing has made me strong and mighty. You've empowered my life for triumph by pouring fresh oil over me.
Psalm 92:10, The Passion Translation

Oil has many uses. Oil lubricates an engine. Oil gushes from the ground. Oil slicks down my hair. Oil makes a baby's skin smooth.

OIL—What's it for?

It's really not what you DO in your life, but what you BECOME in your life that determines how you will flourish.

But we DO so much. And we do it fast!

When you see a light turn yellow do you slow down, speed up or put the pedal to the metal!?

We like to move fast. We are made to GO. But data suggests that busy-ness costs us something. Our ability to listen is now reduced to sound bites and headlines. We feel like we are waiting an eternity as we watch 5 seconds of ads on YouTube. We work fast, eat fast, worship fast, live fast and pray fast. If we want to have a meaningful conversation, we pay a therapist. Why bother cooking and sitting around the table when you can get fast food and eat it on the go?

Sometimes it seems like God is not fast enough for our preferences. Joseph was in prison far too long before he was finally rescued and his dream became reality. Beautiful Esther was sequestered for 12 months, sneaking conversations with her uncle through a chain-link fence. What a waste of time—until she finally speaks to the King, resulting in millions of Jewish lives saved from execution.

Why did it take so long? Why did John the Baptist sit in his jail cell? Couldn't God find a better use of John's time? Why was Paul shipwrecked, put in prison, under house arrest, when he could have been on another amazing mission's trip or planting another church?

My wife and I enjoy an amazing marriage, but it sure took a long time to get there. (Is that too much information?)

My point is this—it's not so much what you do that matters as much as what you are going to become that determines how your life will flourish. Becoming what God intends takes some time!

What if becoming is more important than doing?

I'm reminded of a story where the dad was trying to work, but his four-year-old kept interrupting him. He finally took a page of a magazine with a picture of the world, tore it into little pieces, and directed his son to "put the world together." Thirty minutes later the boy returned with the full puzzle assembled. The father was amazed, "How did you do that so quickly?" The boy answered simply, "There's a picture of a man on the back. When I put the man together, the world came together, too."

You see, God puts the world together as he's putting US together. God intends for us to experience new life, new ideas, new dreams, joy, and strength. He is positioning us to discover unannounced goodness, to recognize treasures yet unseen, and to activate resources yet unused.

Yet there is a problem. NEW requires FRESH! Jesus said, "No one puts new wine in old wineskins." Creating capacity requires process.

Lee Grady, author, says it like this: "The Lord wants to unleash a gushing river of new wine into the church today, but we must prepare our wineskins. What is old must be renewed by the Spirit, what is outdated must be remodeled, and what is ineffective must be replaced. God wants to do a new thing!"

Psalm 92 paints a picture of an overflowing life—a life filled with God perpetually uncovering secrets and bringing victories over enemies, even in old age! FRESH! And the punch line arrives in verse 10:

Your anointing has made me strong and mighty. You've empowered my life for triumph by pouring fresh oil over me.

Anointing is a spectacular word in the Bible. When it was time for a new king in Israel, an unlikely shepherd, David, was selected and anointed with fresh oil by the prophet:

*And the spirit of the Lord came
upon David from that day forward.*
I Samuel 16:13

Pouring oil on David opened an era of new authority, empowering David with a spiritual impartation of the Holy Spirit. David received a supernatural capacity of wisdom to lead as King. Now wars would be won, blessings would be abundant and wisdom would flow. These were not normal times.

Oil did not give him the power to do these things. Rather it gave him the power to become. David killed Goliath because he *became* a giant killer. He wrote psalms because he *became* a worshipper. David led people in the ways of right living because he *became* a good king. The Holy Spirit infused David's life and changed not only what he did, but who he was—what he was becoming!

Psalm 23 records exactly what happened: *You anointed my head with oil!*

Currently I have a beard. But it was becoming wild and scraggly. I was thinking about shaving it until someone suggested I use beard oil. I tried it. It was an undiscovered delight to rub that fragrant oil on my hairy face. It was energizing. I felt like *the most interesting man in the world!*

However, the head is even more important than the beard. When the head is anointed with oil, it signifies a new mindset. The greatest power on this earth is the human mind.

God found no problem overcoming the power of Pharaoh but he never overcame the mindset of the slaves who were in captivity. It took them 40 years in the wilderness to shake off the old mindsets of slavery and enter into freedom.

Paul proclaimed it clearly to the Romans: Even if you know about Jesus, but stay in your old mindset, you'll have no life, no peace. Your carnal mind is an adversary of God.

Oil On Your Head

Fresh oil doesn't just give you power to do things. It actually changes who you are! Holy Spirit anointing can turn you into a flourishing fruit bearer of beautiful strength. Holy Spirit anointing is in life's processes.

You must recognize that anointing comes from the Holy Spirit—the same Holy Spirit who turned David into a King; the same Holy Spirit who anointed Esther to save her people; the same Holy Spirit who descended on Jesus as He was baptized by John.

The power is the same.

Yet we don't see ourselves as capable enough to do anything in our own strength, for our true competence flows from God's empowering presence. He alone makes us adequate ministers who are focused on an entirely new

*covenant. Our ministry is not based on the letter of the law
but through the power of the Spirit.*
II Corinthians 3:5, 6, The Passion Translation

This is where the old and the new collide. Paul is sharing that old relationships with God were built around the law, yet attracted a high level of the Glory of God. Through his excellence and character, God was on display, seen by the people thru the burning bush, the dry path thru the Red Sea and the fallen walls of Jericho.

The Glory of God is God in Action

The Old Testament is filled with God visitations—in the wind; on the mountain; rainbows, earthquakes, lightning. At that time, the commandments were things to DO. *I will be your God but you must keep moral laws—no adultery, murder or lying. Keep the Sabbath. Honor your parents. Have no other Gods.* He gave them a "to do" list, known as the Ten Commandments, so they could get along with each other and honor God. God wanted the best for his people.

The Glory associated with this moment where God visited Moses was so intense, Moses required a veil! There were two reasons for the veil:

1. Moses' face was so bright that it was blinding to look at him.
2. The glory on Moses' face was fading, and he didn't want the people to see the Glory fading from him.

Paul teaches that the new Glory—the Glory of the Holy Spirit—far surpasses the old Glory, and—IT NEVER FADES! It can always be FRESH! The veil is never again needed because it has been removed by Christ. So, the only veil that remains, that could remove you from the Glory (anointing) of God's Spirit is the one that occupies your own carnal mind. The origin of this veil is the enemy—the devil—the God of this Age who wants you to live in your own level of fear, faith, hope and strength.

Comparing the OLD with the NEW

Old (Fading glory) vs New (Freedom)

Freedom is the word we use when we live as God intended. You are free to become a nurturing parent, a strong business leader, an effective teacher, etc. God uniquely formed humans for a personal relationship with Him—to see His face and experience His Glory. With the Old, you do. With the New, you become!

Lovers look at faces, not hands. Remember, Moses asked to see God's face...but he couldn't. It would be too much for him. He might explode. But in the New Covenant, *we can draw close to him with the veil removed.* There are no limitations to intimacy. There are no fading discoveries of love, goodness, kindness or gentleness.

Doing vs Becoming

We all become like mirrors brightly reflecting the glory. We are being transformed into his very image as we move from one brighter level of glory to another. The Holy Spirit has one consistent goal—to change you from conformity to the world and cause you to live the transformed life God created for you.

In this world of doing, doing, doing, the process of becoming and being is ignored or belittled. But in God's glorious economy of anointing, it's in this very process where refinement lies; where the infusion of the spirit takes formation. The world around us gets "fixed" as we become the very essence (glory) of God.

So here's what I want you to do, GOD helping you: Take your everyday, ordinary life—your sleeping, eating, going-to-work, and walking-around life—and place it before GOD as an offering. Embracing what God does for you is the best thing you can do for him. Don't become so well-adjusted to your culture that you fit into it without even thinking. Instead, fix your attention on GOD. You'll be changed from the inside out. Readily recognize what he wants from you, and quickly respond to it. Unlike the culture around you, always dragging you down to its level of immaturity, GOD brings the best out of you, develops well-formed maturity in you.
Romans 12:1, 2, The Message

For a long time I didn't read this clearly. I thought I was supposed to look in the mirror and see me—always occupied, with blemishes, inadequacies, and sin which kept me inglorious. Introspection always leaves you beat up.

But it's not MY face I'm supposed to view! It's the beauty of Jesus!

FRESH OIL Allows You to Become

FRESH oil (anointing) transforms you into:

A COMPETENT MINISTER

He alone makes us adequate ministers who are focused on an entirely new covenant.
II Corinthians 3:6

I see this so clearly in my wife, Becky. She was asked to speak at a state-wide event for women coaches in Texas. God has opened the door for her to be a voice to professional basketball players on a national level. When she first entered this arena of influence, she didn't know where the foul line was on the basketball court (she does now). She's never been an athlete.

But a few years ago, she accepted an invitation to serve three coaches at our local public school, where, year after year, she served donuts and shared from the Bible in a locker room with a bunch of teenage girls who played on the basketball team. She did this for years with no obvious or measurable results... until the Holy Spirit infused those relationships as she shared friendship, brought wisdom in their crises, and manifested the glory of God. Then doors opened for her on the national scene, and she is chaplain of the Dallas women's professional basketball team. Was she wasting her time? I think not.

Fresh anointing made her a spiritual force—a competent minister.

Christians are well-rehearsed in presenting excuses about incompetence. Moses started out—"I stutter. I'm shy. I'm a fugitive." Gideon whined, "I'm the wrong guy. I'm not valiant. I'm the least in my tribe hiding in the winepress." Jeremiah lamented, "I'm a teenage shepherd."

Your excuses are a veil which the fresh oil (anointing) of Christ removes. Your union with the Holy Spirit makes you a competent minister. It just takes one thing to become a minister/servant of God—a mindset change.

Instead he emptied himself of his outward glory by reducing himself to the form of a lowly servant. He became human! He humbled himself and became vulnerable...Because of that

obedience, G<small>OD</small> exalted him and multiplied his greatness!
He has now been given the greatest of all names!
Philippians 2:7-9

Jesus served so the blind could see, the lame could walk, and prisoners would be freed. Change your mind to this: people matter! They matter even when they disagree with you or look different from you.

Jesus' ministry was authoritative, because it was true. It was supernatural, because he was anointed. It was compassionate, because God is love. And it was methodical—He saw needs and met them. Sometimes he fed crowds, healed, taught, cooked fish, turned over tables, kept the nursery...Fresh oil makes you a competent minister—ready to serve and fulfill the needed role.

A CONFIDENT VISIONARY

G<small>OD</small> always makes his grace visible in Christ, who
includes us as partners of his endless triumph. Through our
yielded lives he spreads the fragrance of the knowledge
of G<small>OD</small> everywhere we go.
II Corinthians 2:14

We carry this confidence in our heart
because of our union with Christ.
II Corinthians 3:4

What is visible about God is YOU. Paul says you are the letter He writes now. You are his display. You are proof that His love is real.

Tara, a young woman in our church, decided to show God's love in the public school. She began a program *Inspire*, a ministry in public schools which helps students discover their worth and develop character.

Another young man I know established a ministry to help men who have recently been released from prison, and who need a FRESH start. He provides some new clothes, a place to stay, and help with getting adjusted to their new way of life outside of prison. Simply put, he helps them get back on their feet again, and shares the love of God with them.

Do you carry a vision for spiritual success? Because you don't need the law once a dream is conceived in your heart. Vision is the fuel for the self-discipline required to achieve your dream.

No one tells Serena Williams to practice her serve or eat healthy. She knows that discipline will bring her triumph. And her discipline makes her attractive to sponsors, fans and younger tennis players.

Carry the Dream

It's time to dream again. There is a difference between *having* a dream and *carrying* a dream.

Your responsibility to carry God's dream for you makes accessible and visible the glory, the oil, the FRESH anointing of God. Carry it with you! Dreams without prayer, faithfulness and reliability will never display God. A process is required.

Faith requires a vision. Why did guys march around the walls of a city 7 times? They believed those walls were going to fall down! Why did David pick up 5 stones? He believed at least one of them was going to hit Goliath in the head. Why did the

Early Church stay in the upper room for 10 days? Because they believed that God was going to pour out His spirit on them.

The Holy Spirit gave the dream—and they carried the dream and experienced new Glory.

A GODLY IMAGE

Just as the caterpillar metamorphoses into a butterfly, you are turning into the image of God. The way you live will demonstrate the love of God. The glory of God. The anointing of God. The FRESH OIL of God.

Israel's enemies brought their gods with them into battle. They were adorned with jewels, spices, and other gaudy and flagrant array. They taunted Israel asking, "Where is YOUR God?" But Israel could only answer that their God was invisible. **Israel's God could not be seen, but was always there.**

The difference between the old and the new is that God is visible—in YOU!

✔oil Checkup:

1. What's happening in your life that you can identify the Holy Spirit helping you become what God has in mind?

2. How does gazing/meditating upon the beauty of Jesus impact you?

Night's darkness is dissolving away

as a new day of destiny dawns. So we

must once and for all strip away

what is done in the shadows of darkness,

removing it like filthy clothes.

Romans 13:12

CHAPTER 4

*fr*esh Hope

HOPE: to cherish a desire with anticipation; to desire with expectation of obtainment or fulfillment; to expect with confidence *(Webster's Dictionary)*

I have a morning ritual which includes listening to a particular local radio station. They have a segment on "what's trending" which includes current events, interesting news segments, etc. My heart hurt when I heard suicide was on the list.

During that week Kate Spade and Anthony Bourdain took their own lives. Since then Duffy Fudge (star in Wicked Tuna), Ram Emery (NHL goalkeeper), Billy Knight (UCLA basketball player)...and numerous others have taken their own lives.

Knight's YouTube post: *"I'm lost in life, and I feel like there's no hope. I have no friends with me here. I have no wife, no girlfriend. I have nothing. And I just feel like I cannot continue on..."*

It's of particular concern when celebrities kill themselves, because most of us think famous people have found what everyone is looking for. They live with money, popularity, mansions on islands, etc. When people who have everything fall apart, we tend to wonder if there's any hope for us.

In the previous chapters you have read about "the new"—new ways, love, mercies, resources. Simply put, fresh hearts open up new ways to live! But new always presents a problem—the new cannot be contained in the old. The old wineskins will not be adequate to hold the new wine.

God never changes, but He's new every morning! He presents Himself through undiscovered resources, unseen beauty, and unannounced goodness. But if your mind stays stuck with your old values, order and ideas, you will disqualify yourself from the things you most desire.

Let's look at a famous woman at a well, a favorite Bible story of many. She was fairly young, yet had experienced so much heartache, she was old at heart. She visited the well late in the day so she did not have to interact with the other women. She lived with shame, having already had 5 husbands, and was currently with yet another man. Her heart was empty.

Jesus came along, knowing her past, and offered her something fresh—living water—HOPE! Jesus said, "Try something new." He offered her fresh water for her soul—a new purpose, self-confidence and removal of her shame.

Context is Everything

If I say David killed a man...then tell you he killed an evil giant—the imagery is different. If I say I learned to juggle...then say I learned to juggle on a roller coaster while blindfolded—you have a completely different image.

The old order of priesthood has been set aside as weak and powerless. For the law has never made anyone perfect, but in its place is a far better hope which gives us confidence to experience intimacy with GOD.
Hebrews 7:18

*Now this phrase "once and for all" clearly indicates the final removal of things that are shaking that is the old order, so only what is unshakeable will remain. Since we are receiving our rights to an unshakeable kingdom we should be extremely thankful and offer G*OD *the purest worship that delights his heart as we lay down our lives in absolute surrender, filled with awe.*
Hebrews 12:27, 28

This passage requires a proper context. Early on, they were passionate about worship, overcoming faith, zeal, intimacy with God, caring for one another. But something stalled. They became distracted and disappointed. They still believed in Jesus as Messiah, but they became stale and unsatisfied. They needed some fresh hope.

Think about the context of your life. What's gotten old to you? What did you put hope in that let you down? What shakes you?

Jesus came into your life so old things would pass away and all things would become new. This is not hype or oversell. This is a promise!

See, I do a new thing. Now it springs up. I'm making a way. I'm making streams in the wasteland.
Isaiah 43:19

God's very nature brings new ways to you so your life can grow fresh again with hope! You don't have to settle for stagnation.

So be made strong even in your weakness by lifting up your tired hands in prayer and worship. And strengthen your weak knees for as you keep walking forward on GOD's path all your stumbling ways will be healed!
Hebrews 12:14

Anchors for Your Life

1) **The Cross**—an elaborate unfolding picture of all the old pushed aside—the temple, sacrifices, and legalism.

2) **The Resurrection**—the apex of Jesus' destiny while on earth—makes possible an unshakeable kingdom of living; a hope never experienced before; a revolutionary shift.

Jesus did not come only as a Lamb sacrificed for sin. He came to establish a new dominion, new government, new ways, a new kingdom. When you know about the cross and you know about the kingdom He brought, that's the basis of new hope every day for you.

When a team hires a new coach, a company hires a new CEO, or a city elects a new mayor, you expect new values, new powers and new outcomes. A new coach might emphasize conditioning, and institute sprints or weight-lifting. The players might complain, not wanting to change and preferring the old ways. But that presents the problem—they want the trophy but want to continue in their old patterns and routines. That new coach just might say, "You can't put a new championship into an old wineskin."

This is why Jesus came to earth—to abolish old values, old powers and old outcomes which keep us limited and inadequate. Dying on the cross, rising from death, and releasing the Holy Spirit was for this purpose—so everything could change—to make the world new! Jesus brought hope to the world!

The most daring claim Jesus ever made was that He was going to bring a new Kingdom to earth, and that this new Kingdom would be the basis of your hope. The Kingdom comes because God loves us but it accelerates as we receive it.

Kingdom is a Process

Since we are receiving our rights to an unshakeable kingdom we should be extremely thankful and offer GOD the purest worship that delights his heart...
Hebrews 12:28

Night's darkness is dissolving away as a new day of destiny dawns. So we must once and for all strip away what is done in the shadows of darkness, removing it like filthy clothes.
Romans 13:12

Paul uses an image here that reminds me of my childhood. He says that the kingdom is like 5:30 am...just before sunrise... when you can barely see the trees, animals...just a grey light.

When my mother would come into my room and say "Time to wake up!" I would respond, "Be right there..." then roll over two or three times. After a while dad would come in. "Jim Hennesy, do you know what time it is? It's time to get out of bed. Wake up!"

It's time to wake up! And get up! Time for a new outlook—a new authority in your life. You cannot see everything clearly yet, but you can see a little light, a little goodness, a little love coming in. Evil isn't gone but a few demons are being defeated. Sickness and death are not completely removed but there are healings, miracles and displays of God.

I haven't yet seen the removal of racism and hatred, but I can see God's love displayed through my congregation and others around the world.

New hope comes with a new king! **Acceleration of the kingdom involves your willingness to receive it.**

Kingdom is Contrasted

And who would light a lamp and then hide it in an obscure place? Instead, it's placed where everyone in the house can benefit from its light.
Matthew 7:15

So if the tree is good, it will produce good fruit; but if the tree is bad, it will bear only rotten fruit and it deserves to be cut down and burned.
Matthew 7:17-19

Everyone who hears my teaching and applies it to his life can be compared to a wise man who built his house on an unshakable foundation. When the rains fell and the flood came, with fierce winds beating upon his house it stood firm because of its strong foundation.

But everyone who hears my teaching and does not apply it to his life can be compared to a foolish man who built his house on sand. When it rained and rained and the flood came, with wind and waves beating upon his house, it collapsed and was swept away.
Matthew 7:24-27, The Passion Translation

When Jesus explained the unshakeable kingdom, he utilized the "compare and contrast" method. Two trees, side by side—they look the same but one bears fruit, the other is for firewood. Two lights—both send lumens, but one is hidden under a bowl where the light cannot be seen. Two houses—same neighborhood, same floorplan—one stands firm in the storm and the other collapses in the wind.

This is quite a shocking teaching. I used to think the contrast was good people compared to bad people. Moral versus immoral. Kids in high school involved in sex and drugs compared to those who go to church.

Contrast is not what you think. It's not the wicked versus church members. It is the OLD versus the NEW!

When you read in the Bible about people in the kingdom and those outside the kingdom, you can barely tell the difference. Both groups worshipped, prayed, gave offerings and studied the scriptures. What distinguished the groups had little to do with external behavior, economic standing or big sins compared to little sins. Frankly, even today, you cannot tell by looking at someone who is living in the OLD and who is living in the NEW.

Not everyone who says to me LORD, LORD will enter the kingdom of heaven...on the day of judgment many will say 'LORD, don't you remember us? Didn't we prophesy in your name? Didn't we cast out demons in your name?' But I will have to say to them, go away from me, rebels. I have never been joined to you.
Matthew 7:21

Wait! Isn't this how we measure spiritual success—those who prophesy, pray, cast out demons, lead worship?

Now this kind of thinking might not be your fault. You might have been taught the kingdom of God was keeping a set of rules, but Jesus makes it very clear. The key to new hope and living the life we were made to live, in union with him and his purposes for us, is to merge our life into His.

This is why it was so easy for desperate people—people with no hope—tax collectors, prostitutes, the immoral—to embrace what the Messiah was offering—HOPE! They had tried it their way and it was a disaster. Religious people, on the other hand, had little interest in Jesus. They were satisfied with their world, settling for so much less.

Exodus 19 (and repeated in Hebrew 12) paints a dramatic scene for the Hebrews. Instead of heading toward the "land of milk and honey" that God promised, the Hebrews crossed over the Red Sea and turned the wrong way. Their complaining was unending—no food, the weather...in fact, some said it was better when they were slaves in Egypt! But God said, *"Trust Me!"*

You have seen what I did to Egypt and how I carried you on eagles' wings and brought you to me. If you will listen obediently to what I say and keep my covenant, out of all peoples you'll be

my special treasure. The whole Earth is mine to choose from, but you're special: a kingdom of priests, a holy nation.
Exodus 19:4, 5

*You have seen what I did...*His Grace and His love was manifest—they didn't do anything! They were carried on wings of love.

*Now if you will obey Me and keep My covenant...*He didn't say **make** a covenant, but **keep** the covenant by obeying.

Notice the order of his admonition. **You cannot obey your way into His presence.** His order is grace first—He rescues us, then keeping the covenant follows. God does His part first.

After church, invariably Beck and I are on our way to eat at a restaurant and ask each other where to eat. "I don't know, you choose." "No, you choose." Then, I suggest somewhere I think *she* will want to eat. Why? Because when you love someone, you prefer their will over yours.

It's the same way with God. We prefer His ways over our own—they are better and bigger—once we have embraced His new Kingdom and all it has to offer. And the result of obeying and keeping the covenant is:

1) **personal treasure**—we belong exclusively to Him

2) **kingdom of priests**—He gives us authority and influence

3) **holy nation status**—He brings His revolutionary ways into our earthly life

One of my great concerns with believers today is they might attend a church, serve on a committee, follow the rules, even cast out demons, but miss the essence of experiencing all God planned for them.

In the new kingdom, He is our source. He is our liberator.

In a recent study published in the journal, *Emotion,* researchers asked hundreds of people over 50 to name their single biggest regret in life. Over 76% gave one top answer—they didn't fulfill their *ideal* self. They didn't pursue becoming the person they would *like* to be. As believers, I think we could agree that we truly want to become all that God has in mind for us.

The Hebrews lost confidence because they lost sight of the grace of God. They were obeying Him, but without worship or gratitude for God, who had already delivered them from their enemies.

Kingdom is Relational

Since we are receiving our rights to the unshakeable kingdom we should be extremely thankful and offer GOD the purest worship that delights his heart.
Hebrews 12:28

The secret to fresh hope is first, a relationship with God— living with the awareness of His Goodness, His presence.

The astounding phenomena Moses witnessed caused him to shudder with fear and he could only say, "I am trembling in terror!"
Hebrews 12:21

Why is there so much shaking going on in this story? Moses was shaking. The mountain was shaking. There was fire and smoke and the earth rocked at the sound of God's voice from the mountain.

Why did Peter say, "Depart from me?" Why did Isaiah say, "Woe is me!" Job saw God in a whirlwind, and Ezekiel went kind of crazy looking at the glory of God. What was happening?

In the presence of someone greater than ourselves, we shrivel and shake.

Most people build their self-image on some form of virtue—"I'm not perfect but I'm pretty good. I'm basically a good guy. I know I did a terrible thing but that's not who I am." The essence of the Old is that people assume their virtue is the basis of their hope—if I am good, people will like me and God will bless me.

But in His Presence, our virtue collapses.

God's new kingdom brings HOPE because of relationship with Him. God is terrifying, but he wants YOU. Your hope is not in the old, unapproachable separation of God. Your hope is at the mountain of grace, truth, and forgiveness.

The story of the prodigal son clearly defines hope. The son wanted the father's blessing without a relationship. The result of that decision was not good—the son became homeless and was eating leftovers from pigs. He returned home because he could—he knew the character of his father. And there his father stood with arms opened wide to welcome him back. Hope restored. Fresh hope.

The gospel of the Kingdom is not about behavior modification. It's about relationship with Father God. If you want the blessing without the relationship, it won't turn out good for you.

About 18 months before my father passed away, he received an unexpected medical report that wasn't good. I asked him, "Are you afraid?" He answered strongly, "No. I'm at peace."

How did he live at peace in such a shaky and unpredictable time in his life? He had hope. Hope in God. Understanding of His Goodness. Clarity about his relationship with God. His joy came from an overflow of intimacy with God and a radical expectation of a future with Him. He knew he had a Father who loved him. My father, even at the age of 82, had fresh HOPE!

✔ hope Checkup:

1. Identify the areas of life where you could use new hope.

2. How is the Kingdom of God "dawning" in your life currently?

We look away from the natural realm

and we fasten our gaze

onto Jesus who birthed faith

within us and who leads

us forward into faith's perfection.

Hebrews 12:2, The Passion Translation

CHAPTER 5

*fr*esh Holiness

HOLINESS: Other; not of this world;
perfect, immeasurable, incomparable.

This chapter is dedicated to everyone who runs races—racing to work, racing to soccer games, racing home and racing to dinner...the rat race!

Most Americans who grew up in the USA memorized the poem, "In 1492 Columbus sailed the ocean blue..." We learned that instead of finding a trade route to Asia, his trip unleashed unimaginable possibilities in the imagination of Europeans—a new world! Suddenly, anything seemed possible.

Ponce de Leon heard of a mythical island, Bimini, where a spring of water flowed, and whoever drank of it was forever young. King Ferdinand financed the trip, but the spring was never found. Instead, he found Florida.

El Dorado, the Lost City of Gold, teased explorers with hopes of unfathomable riches. Alas, Belalcazar searched for three years in the jungles of Columbia, all to no avail.

But failures did not discourage those with adventure in their veins. What motivated all of these obsessions was the possibility of something that had yet to be discovered.

We aren't much different. How many wives lose their husbands to NFL ticket or poker games because watching football or winning a $20 pot may be as close as they will get to real adventure? They want to get as close to it as possible, hoping to discover some quality of life, something yet undiscovered.

Others try to overcome disappointing life circumstances through children, exercise routines, romance novels, or careers. I'm talking about desires deeply embedded in us, urging us to run races, but, seemingly, never getting us across the finish line.

People fit into three categories:

1. those dead in their souls and divorced from all desires,
2. those who are addicted, and
3. those who are alive, but thirsty for new and fresh.

God promises something to satisfy the deepest longings of the human heart!

Before you lies undiscovered resources, unseen beauty and unannounced goodness—new ways to live in the freshness of God—holiness!

Now, for some of you, holiness is a tough concept. In 1970, David Wilkerson made a movie, "The Cross and the Switchblade." I really wanted to see it, but, at that time, my religious circle did not allow us to go to a movie theatre. It was an unholy place. In that day, Beck (my wife) could only wear dresses to school...and the length of her skirt mattered greatly at the college where we attended. Beck's mom was so "holy" that she didn't wear make-up...until she started selling it! Because then, holy changed. With rules and regulations being rewritten over time, it's complicated to keep up with what is holy and what is unholy.

We need to discover true holiness because *"without holiness, we cannot see God!"* Hebrews 12:14

Holiness is not deadness. It is passion! Holiness is not divorcing yourself from your desires, put there by God, but being attuned to them. Paying attention to what you truly were created for and put on this earth to do—that's holiness. We honestly don't actually know what will satisfy those longings. And that's why we need God's help—a new mindset. A fresh wineskin.

In I Samuel, chapters 21 and 22, David is a fugitive, running to escape King Saul. There is a bounty on his head. He knows for certain that King Saul's dark moods, jealousy and hatred toward him will not pass. David finds himself without food and out of ideas. I'm sure he thought he should just give up on the idea of being king.

Have you thought about just giving up on your dreams, your marriage, your kids, or your God-breathed destiny? This is the time you should run to the holy place. David found his.

A Priest and a Sanctuary

Definition: Sanctuary—a consecrated place; a place of refuge and protection.

Sanctuary is a place for holiness. Holy is a Bible word to describe "otherness" (matchlessness, purity, beauty) of God. It doesn't have to be a church building. It's wherever God actually meets humans. Holiness was in the burning bush and at Mt. Sinai with Moses. The three Hebrew children found holiness in a fiery furnace. Wherever God infuses you with "otherness" is your sanctuary. It's where we find Him.

If it's merely human, it's not holy.

God is so "other" that it causes problems. Peter fished all his life. Fishing was the family business, yet Jesus showed him holy fishing—in the middle of the day (the wrong time of day to go fishing) and in deep water—catching more fish than the net could contain. You would think Peter would celebrate with Jesus, but just the opposite occurred. Peter begged Jesus to leave him alone.

> *When Simon Peter saw this astonishing miracle, he knelt at Jesus' feet and begged him, "Go away from me, Master, for I am a sinful man!"*
> Luke 5:8 (TPT)

Isaiah, a regular worshipper, one day saw the Lord high and lifted up, and was so overwhelmed he cried, "Woe is me! Depart from me!" He had seen Holy. When Jesus brought holy peace to the disciples sinking ship, they were more scared of the calm than the lightning and thunder. "Other" scares us.

Ivy League schools have huge depression rates because, all of a sudden, smart kids meet someone smarter. All their lives they've heard "You're so smart," yet now, they are making C's in class. When you meet the "other" level of smart, your perception faces a reality check.

We as human beings face our own reality. We are pretty good. We are OK. But when we meet God, our virtue collapses. Our pre-conceived notion of goodness falls apart when we encounter holiness. This is one of the main reasons why holy gets redefined as a set of rules to obey, rather than God's infusion of His supernatural life into us.

C.S. Lewis describes it this way: *We are not made to live as half-hearted creatures fooling around with food and drink when infinite joy is offered. Like an ignorant child making mud pies in a slum because you can't imagine what is meant by a holiday at sea.* The problem is we were made for holy, but when we get close to holy, we feel small. So we choose to deny our desires, reject our hunger for holy, and play with the mud pies.

People attend movies all the time, looking for holiness/other. Our connection to the screen is the feeling we get when good overcomes evil or death is escaped. This is the life we long for. Life that never ends. The good guy always wins. Love that lasts forever. This is the life of holiness!

We embrace holy when we visit the sanctuary.

David went to Nob, to Ahimelech the Priest. Ahimelech was alarmed as he went out to greet David: "What are you doing here all by yourself—and not a soul with you?"

David answered Ahimelech the Priest, "The king sent me on a mission and gave strict orders: 'This is top secret—not a word of this to a soul.' I've arranged to meet up with my men in a certain place. Now, what's there here to eat? Do you have five loaves of bread? Give me whatever you can scrounge up!"
I Samuel 21:1-3

David burst into the holy place. At this point, the only thing on his mind was survival. But he was about to get so much more. David's dreams were under attack. The path he imagined toward becoming King was falling apart.

The priest, Ahimelech, was going about his duties in the priestly way—orderly, predictable and well-planned. Suddenly, David, the future king, blasts unexpectedly into this reverent space. "What are you doing here, David?" Ahimelech inquired. David lies, "I'm on a mission for the king. My men need food."

Are you disappointed in David and his lying? He's not in the story to teach morality; he's in the Book to show us how holy comes to the wilderness. David lies, but he doesn't quit. He doesn't stop running when the race gets hard.

"I don't have any regular bread on hand," said the priest.
"I only have holy bread. If your men have not
slept with women recently, it's yours."
I Samuel 21:4

The only food in the sanctuary was holy bread—bread set apart for communion. For priests in that time, the bread of presence was set out each week as an offering to God. Twelve loaves of fresh bread, one on each altar, on the Sabbath. At the end of each week, the priests, and only the priests, could eat the old bread.

David said, "None of us has touched a woman. I always do it
this way when I'm on a mission: My men abstain from sex.
Even when it is an ordinary mission we do that—
how much more on this holy mission."

So the priest gave them the holy bread. It was the only bread
he had, Bread of the Presence that had been removed from
GOD'S presence and replaced by fresh bread
at the same time.
I Samuel 21:5, 6

David argued he was on a mission, authorized by the king, and he was hungry. So Ahimelech bent the rules and gave the holy bread to David.

David asked Ahimelech, "Do you have a spear or sword of any kind around here? I didn't have a chance to grab my weapons. The king's mission was urgent and I left in a hurry."

The priest said, "The sword of Goliath, the Philistine you killed at Oak Valley—that's here! It's behind the Ephod wrapped in a cloth. If you want it, take it. There's nothing else here."

"Oh," said David, "there's no sword like that! Give it to me!" And at that, David shot out of there, running for his life from Saul.
I Samuel 21:8-11

David would not survive without a weapon. And the only sword available was Goliath's sword, displayed as a shrine for others to come and reflect on what God had done. It certainly was of no use currently behind a glass for viewing! David grabbed it.

David came to hide, eat bread, and grab a sword—strength for the day and weapon for the fight. Swords and bread are metaphors for God's Word throughout the Bible. David came to the holy place empty, but left full and equipped. Holy places have what is required for holy living.

Irony of the Holy Place

One of Saul's officials was present that day keeping a religious vow. His name was Doeg the Edomite. He was chief of Saul's shepherds.

David shot out of there, running for his life from Saul. He went to Achish, king of Gath. When the servants of Achish saw him, they said, "Can this be David, the famous David? Is this the one

*they sing of at their dances? Saul kills by the thousand,
David by the ten thousand!"*

*When David realized that he had been recognized, he panicked,
fearing the worst from Achish, king of Gath. So right there, while
they were looking at him, he pretended to go crazy, pounding
his head on the city gate and foaming at the mouth, spit dripping
from his beard. Achish took one look at him and said to his servants, "Can't you see he's crazy? Why did you let him in here?
Don't you think I have enough crazy people to put up with as it is
without adding another? Get him out of here!"*
I Samuel 21:7, 11-15

Doeg was in the shadows, watching David lie, eat holy bread
and take Goliath's sword. He knew the background between
David and Saul. And he knew this inside information would
turn useful with King Saul. His fortune was about to change.
Once Saul heard the news...

*The king said, "Death, Ahimelech! You're going to die—
you and everyone in your family!"*

*The king ordered his henchmen, "Surround and kill the priests
of GOD! They're hand in glove with David. They knew he was
running away from me and didn't tell me." But the king's men
wouldn't do it. They refused to lay a hand on the priests of GOD.*

*Then the king told Doeg, "You do it—massacre the priests!"
Doeg the Edomite led the attack and slaughtered the priests, the
eighty-five men who wore the sacred robes. He then carried the*

massacre into Nob, the city of priests, killing man and woman, child and baby, ox, donkey, and sheep—the works.
I Samuel 22:16-20

The entire village was slaughtered, save one son of the priest, Abiathar. There is an irony in the holy place. Both David and Doeg were there. David found strength and courage but Doeg found something which turned him into a villain.

LESSONS LEARNED

Instead of quitting, look for a sanctuary

There is more to see and to find than the world knows about.

We look away from the natural realm and we fasten our gaze onto Jesus who birthed faith within us and who leads us forward into faith's perfection.
Hebrews 12:2, The Passion Translation

Holy is an infusion of focus. Holiness moves us from what we think is going on to actual reality.

Two famous things happened in Dothan. In II Kings 6, Elisha's servant reports one minute that they are surrounded by chariots and horses, ready for slaughter. The next minute, his eyes were opened to the holy, and he saw God's angel army.

Dothan was also where Joseph's brothers stripped him, put him in a pit, and sold him to the Arabs travelling through to Egypt. Joseph had a dream. But his race took him through rejection, betrayal and incarceration. Yes, it was unfair. The transformation took a long path through unfair circumstances and loneliness. But through the process, Joseph's soul was breaking open to the holy. Joseph had to look away from the natural, and focus on the holy of God's destiny for his life.

Holy places make you better or worse

So be made strong even in your weakness by lifting up your tired hands in prayer and worship. And strengthen your weak knees, for as you keep walking forward on GOD's paths all your stumbling ways will be divinely healed!

In every relationship be swift to choose peace over competition, and run swiftly toward holiness, for those who are not holy will not see the Lord.
Hebrews 12:12-14

Wonderful things happen in holy places. We see God and discover His love, his provision and his weapons. We experience a power surge.

Terrible things happen in holy places. Doeg used the holy place to insulate his heart, strengthen his sense of superiority, get an advantage over the competition and justify the king's hatred of David. He walked away from the holy place and used what he had learned to advance his own cause.

It's possible to be near Jesus, see the communion bread and remember the victory over Goliath, yet leave with a harder heart. Cold-hearted people can resist His mercies and embrace their own self-sufficiencies. Desperate people embrace holy.

Holy places make old things new

Goliath's sword was repurposed to be used by God. David arrived at the sanctuary in weakness and desperation. When he left, trouble wasn't gone. Saul was still after him, and, in some ways, the threat was more intense. But David carried bread for strength to his army and the sword to fight. This brought assurance and hope to his followers. They knew they were going to make it.

There was a day when pots and pans were holy; bells around horses' necks were holy; the temple was holy. There is actually no limitation to holy places. Your house can be holy. Your school, your marriage...every circumstance of life, a conversation or a shopping trip can encounter holy. God's love, beauty, courage, strength and revelation are just waiting on you. Transformation is available to you.

✔ holiness Checkup:

1. In what personal circumstance have you found the holiness of God?

2. How does God manifest His holiness to you? How does He speak to your soul?

We look away from the natural realm

and we fasten our gaze

onto Jesus who birthed faith

within us and who leads

us forward into faith's perfection.

Hebrews 12:2, The Passion Translation

CHAPTER 6

*fr*esh Attitude

ATTITUDE: Predisposition of life created by perception, belief and experience which highly influences success.

We've all heard the story of the little boy who was ushered into a room filled with a pile of manure. He walked in, grabbed a shovel, and declared, "There must be a pony in here somewhere!"

That's an inspiring attitude. I must admit, I'm not *naturally* that little boy. But I do recognize the importance of my attitude—especially as I lead people—on my leadership team, in my congregation, my family and others I may influence.

A new attitude releases new authority in your life.

The confidence of my calling enables me to overcome every difficulty without shame, for I have an intimate revelation of this God. And my faith in Him convinces me that He is more than able to keep all that I've placed in His hands safe and secure until the fullness of His appearing.
II Timothy 1:12, The Passion Translation

*For God has not given us a spirit of fear, but
of power and of love and of a sound mind.*
II Timothy 1:7, New King James Version

Why is the lion the king of the jungle? He's not the
smartest, fastest, strongest or biggest. Yet, when the lion roars,
others tremble. His roar sends all other animals scampering.
The elephant is much stronger. When an elephant sees the lion
he thinks he is in for a bad day. But when the lion encounters
the elephant he instinctively is planning to eat it for lunch. The
lion is king of the jungle because he views himself as king of
the jungle! His attitude defines his dominion in the jungle.

Remember, new things come to fresh hearts. God has so
much new for you—new ways, new power, new anointing and
new love. But the new only comes to a fresh mindset. Jesus
told us not to put old wine into new wineskins. It won't work.
Your faith can get brittle. Your love can get old. Your joy can
grow stale. Your dreams become fatigued. There remains unannounced goodness, undiscovered resources, and unseen glo-
ries ahead. God has not fully disclosed all He has for you. But
without a new mindset, your heart will never be able to receive
the new.

One of the books toward the end of the New Testament is
Hebrews. It's the story of Jewish believers who accepted the
fact that Jesus was the Son of God, and their Messiah. But confidence was a problem for the Jewish believers. At first, the
gospel was clear to them, and even activity of the Spirit. Yet
their access to His presence and the wondrous miracles He performed wasn't quite enough for them. Something caused them
to feel victimized and overwhelmed with life. They seemed
poised to stop. To quit. They were not enthusiastic anymore.
They were simply waiting.

Abraham received a promise and waited...until he and Sarah were so old, pregnancy seemed impossible. David received a promise and waited...all the while being chased around the wilderness. He wasn't wasting his time. His heart was being conditioned for the assignment ahead of him. Moses wanted to deliver his people, but waited for forty years. During that time, his soul was broken open and he learned meekness. Joseph received a dream and waited...the pit, prison, Potiphar's wife, and finally the palace! You are no different.

Why is greatness always preceded by waiting? Because it is in the waiting where attitudes are formed, and the atmosphere—mind, body, soul and heart—for greatness is established.

The LION and the EAGLE

God only identifies himself with two animals—the lion and the eagle. If you are going to rule the jungle or soar above the clouds, you can't think of yourself as a hyena or a grasshopper. Your attitude must align with your design. What are your physical, emotional, relational, and spiritual strengths?

Focus on the strengths God has given you. Don't lose confidence. Don't give up! You may be one day or one month away from greatness and a new heart awakening. Attitude is a direct result of what you believe! Actually, attitude is a direct result of in Whom you believe!

Paul states, "I know in whom I have believed and am persuaded that He is able to keep what I have committed to him until that day." If you only have a "what" to believe in, you lose loyalty, perspective and perseverance. But if you have a personal relationship with a King, a Savior, a risen Prince of Peace, that is the confidence you need to stay the course.

Recently I was ministering at another church. I was scheduled to speak for three sessions—the first one was ok. The second session I was brilliant—I felt God using me. But there was no "amen" in the heart of the people. They weren't receiving my words well. I had one more session left. Prayerfully, I questioned, "Where's the gap?" Immediately, the thought, ATTITUDE, came into my spirit. They didn't believe they could roar or soar. They didn't believe they carried spiritual authority. They didn't believe they could steward the presence of the Almighty. My words did not resonate because of their existing mindset.

For twenty-four years I've spoken at the orientation at the beginning of the school year to our Christian school teachers and staff. After an hour or two I can predict which teachers will succeed. It's hardly ever the smartest, the cutest, or the one who prays the loudest or the most—it's the ones who present a good attitude who will ultimately succeed.

God Created YOU to Succeed!

Write this upon your heart—God created you to succeed! Theologians call it the "dominion mandate." In the same way we're not surprised when birds fly, fish swim or seeds bloom, God has ordained and designed you, his human creation, to flourish, prosper, bear fruit and overcome obstacles.

Your attitude is deeply powerful. If you want something new, a fresh attitude is essential.

Jesus Encounters His Father's Announcement

Jesus had the attitude of a lion—the Lion of Judah is one of the names He called himself.

One day he found his cousin, John, baptizing. He walked out of hiding and asked his cousin to baptize him. Suddenly out of heaven a voice came, "This is my beloved Son..." and attitudes shifted. At that pivotal moment, Jesus received affirmation (although he had not performed any miracles yet); affection (His father God called him beloved); acceptance (my son); and anointing (the resource to fulfill his mission).

God announced affirmation, affection, acceptance and anointing upon Jesus. What did the Father do for Jesus that He has not done for you? Christians know the same voice of Father affirmation.

Of course, Satan saw it all! He unleashed a plot to discourage Jesus. On the mount of temptation he blatantly challenged Jesus, "If you are the son of God, command these stones..." This was a direct attempt to assault Jesus' attitude.

But the next scene is Jesus' attitude scene! Jesus goes to the synagogue, the regular place for community worship and roars:

God's Spirit is on me; he's chosen me to preach the Message of good news to the poor, sent me to announce pardon to prisoners and recovery of sight to the blind, to set the burdened and battered free, to announce, "This is God's year to act!"

*He rolled up the scroll, handed it back to the assistant,
and sat down. Every eye in the place was on him, intent.
Then he started in, "You've just heard Scripture make history.
It came true just now in this place."*
Luke 4:18-20, The Passion Translation

**MINDSET: I am about to make a difference! I am about to
display significance!**

It is not arrogant for you to awaken to your spiritual significance. In fact, the very act of acceptance opens the door for a fresh attitude, and an authority in your identity, purpose and value.

Our church recently received direct revelation from one of our guest speakers, Dr. Joseph Garlington. He was preaching, and simply stated "Jesus is coming to this place." Smack—electricity! Holy Spirit presence was tangible and recognizable.

But on Monday morning I woke up, and Beck wasn't paying enough attention to me. The offerings were down. The car needed repair. It was a bad day. I had to fight for the right attitude.

Yes, the devil can be a problem. But he is not capable of taking away your affirmation, acceptance, anointing, or diluting God's affection toward you. He can only assault your attitude.

Satan customizes his temptations. In fact, he used his knowledge about Jesus to offer temptations where he thought Jesus might be most vulnerable. He offered bread to Him since he was fasting for 40 days and was quite hungry, I'm sure. Satan knows a lot about you, too, and where you are most vulnerable.

POTENTIAL ATTITUDE KILLERS

Discontentment

*I have learned whatever state I am in to be content. I can
do all things through Christ who strengthens me.*
Philippians 4:11, 13

Contentment and confidence go together. Contentment is not complacency. Contentment feeds the right attitude. Contentment is a satisfaction, a peace where you are, on your way to your promise. Contentment must be learned and exercised. Paul's attitude was, "I can do..." He's not talking about performance. He is testifying to a grace that sustains him in any circumstance.

Recently Beck was trolling through social media and came across a celebrity with whom we were acquainted, who had moved to Dallas. He didn't visit our church. He chose another church. Beck said it seems like high-level influencers choose to go there. Quick attitude check, "God, why do all the pretty people, all the money, all the influencers...why can't I preach like him, be taller, be skinnier, have better friends..."

Then I came across Psalm 131:

*Lord my heart is meek before you. I don't consider myself
better than others. I'm content to not pursue matters that are
over my head, things I'm not ready yet to understand.
I am humbled and quieted in your presence like a
contented child who rests on his mother's lap.*

Your attitude of success requires you to learn not to chafe under God-imposed limitations. That's where all the trouble began. Adam and Eve, with only one God-imposed limitation, whined, "If we can't have that...God must not love us..."

Contentment is intentionally practiced and learned.

Loneliness (Isolation)

King David was blessed. He conquered most of his enemies. He was popular. He drew significance from winning battles. He was a warrior. One spring he decided to stay home, and that's when he saw Bathsheba bathing on the rooftop. He used his position to seduce her and conspire to murder her husband, causing much unnecessary pain.

When loneliness comes it sounds like this: "I wish someone understood me. I need encouragement. I wish I had one friend I could rely on." You've been there. I know I have. If you lose sight of your significance, you set yourself up for failure.

God engineers us for specific expressions of His glory. He places us in venues where the glory of God flows through our hands, feet and mouth. Beck recently noticed a homeless couple while we were eating at a local restaurant. I promise, she sounded like Jesus as she spoke to them and ministered hope and life to them.

If you are not aware of your purpose, you miss those opportunities. When you isolate yourself and detach from the things God assigned for you, you begin to feel misunderstood, and the spiral of self-pity begins. Then comes a loss of balance in your life and feelings of insignificance. Not long after, bad ideas come along.

A successful attitude requires an awareness of belonging—longing to be. Significance comes from belonging. "This is my beloved son!" A persevering attitude requires defining to Whom you belong. You belong to God. You belong to your family. You belong to the world. You belong here on earth.

Conformity

Do not be conformed to this world, but be transformed by the renewing of your mind that you may prove what is the good and perfect and acceptable will of GOD.
Romans 12:2

There is always outside pressure to fit in. But your greatness requires occasional extraction from group-think. The world pressures, "If you're not like us, think like us, look like us, desire things we desire, wear the right clothes, buy the right car...something is wrong with you."

What if something is wrong with them?

The only conformity you should desire is conformity to the image of the Son of God. That's enough to work on the rest of your life. If you conform to any other image, you will never create. If you walk on established paths only, you will never make a new one. My temptation is to behave a certain way, to make praise more palatable, and tone down spiritual gifts. But I don't think it's arrogance to say, God wants you to be you. He wants you to grow your potential. Being who you are and who He made you to be brings great glory to your creator, God.

Inattentiveness

Be sober, vigilant (watchful) because your adversary the devil prowls around like a roaring lion seeking whom he may devour. Resist him.
I Peter 5:8

Recently my daughter, Katee, mentioned millennials aren't coming to our church like they used to. I had not noticed. She made a few suggestions. We discussed it back and forth. I realized I had become inattentive to the atmosphere, the impression we were making in the foyer, the parking lot, and the sanctuary. I had fallen into organizational inertia—letting it just run itself. Someone must be attentive to the worship, the children, the millennials and the spiritual life of our congregation. And that someone was ME.

Watch is a spiritual command! Watch your words. Watch your testimony. Watch over your friends. Be attentive to your soul.

Could you not watch with me for one hour?
Matthew 26:40

Watch out for the devil. Watchfulness is an attitude that perseveres and keeps confidence high. Have you ever observed a coach on the sideline? He is ever watchful of not only what his team is doing, but what the other team (enemy) is doing—anticipating his next move to defend the tactics of the opposing team. That's watchfulness.

Ingratitude

Without gratitude, a spirit of scarcity seeps in. "I can't do it. I don't have enough to be generous." The attitude of getting rather than receiving creeps in. "I'll get this for myself. I can make this happen." If you want to live with pressure, get an attitude that says, "If it happens, I have to make it happen!"

Gratitude is the gateway into His abiding presence.

*You can pass through His open gates with the password
of praise. Come right into His presence with thanksgiving.
Come bring your thank offering to him and
affectionately bless His beautiful name!*
Psalm 100:4, The Passion Translation

This is where His presence resides.

*The weapons of our warfare are not carnal, but mighty
in G*OD *for pulling down strongholds. Casting down
arguments and every high thing that exalts itself
against the knowledge of God, bringing every thought
into captivity to the obedience of Christ.*
II Corinthians 10:4

A stronghold is a place of strength, either for the kingdom of God, or the kingdom of evil. The precursor of a damaging stronghold is a wrong attitude. If you belong to God, you are in a war zone. From Paul's perspective, an evil stronghold was old thinking—believing a lie as if it were truth.

You can be a dynamic believer and still have strongholds in your life. We all live with strongholds—those areas of life where we are tempted to believe the lies of the enemy. The narrative sounds like: "I'll never succeed as a pastor of a large church...I'll never have a strong marriage...We will never be happy..."

For many years Beck and I believed the narrative that we had married the wrong person. We just weren't the "right one" for each other. But that was a LIE! We were listening to the wrong voice and had begun to believe the deception. The day we recognized that voice came from the deceiver, we positioned ourselves to have a strong and vibrant life together, serving each other and the Kingdom with our strengths as a couple.

Don't let the enemy exploit those seeds of a wrong attitude. Those attitudes of fear, lust, greed, unforgiveness or bitterness can become a stronghold. But you can break free from those strongholds of the enemy. It is not a matter of "getting a better attitude." I'm telling you today to replace the lies with the truth! His grace is sufficient. His love is everlasting. His goodness and His power is your birthright!

✔ attitude Checkup

1. Do you see yourself as a loser and a victim, or as a winner and a leader? Your perception of yourself matters. How did you gain your perception?

2. Do you think of yourself as a random life, living without an assignment? Or do you wake up in the morning with a mission, a passion, and a reason for living? Your purpose matters.

3. Where do you turn for value? The source of your significance matters.

Ask yourself these questions, and truthfully evaluate where you are right now.

He was unable to do any

great miracle in Nazareth,

except to heal a few sick

people by laying his hands

upon them.

Mark 6:5

CHAPTER 7

*fr*esh Perspective

by Robert Madu

PERSPECTIVE: a particular attitude toward or
way of regarding something; a point of view.

I absolutely, positively love my job. I think I have the greatest job on planet earth—preaching the good news of the Gospel. I am created to do what I do!

But there is a difference between a job and a calling. A job is what you are *paid* to do. A calling is what you were *created* to do.

My mother told me that, as a kid, I would be toddling around in my diaper sing-songing, "I'm gonna to be a preacher. I'm gonna to be a preacher!" I would preach to my stuffed animals until they repented.

Even though I understand now that God has a mandate on my life to preach the infallible Word of God, it's was very clear that God did not need ME to speak to people. When God wants to speak to you, he can speak through EVERYTHING! Not just the worship song, the preacher, or a book. He will speak to you through EVERYTHING! Through your circumstances, through your spouse, situation, kids, job...

God speaks in surround sound.

I learned this very quickly. My wife, Taylor, doesn't like to go to the movies with me because God speaks to me at the movie theatre—throughout the entire movie. Shakespeare said, "God speaks in stones." Recently, God spoke to me in the bathroom at the airport.

I was travelling from New York to Tulsa. When I arrived in Tulsa, I thought the airport was closed. There were people inside, but the doors were shut. I kept walking. Doors were shut. All of a sudden, I decided to take one more step forward, and automatically, supernaturally, the doors opened.

I went to the bathroom. The faucets were off, too. I thought to myself, what kind of ghetto bathroom is this?!? Then I placed my hands under the faucet. Water started flowing automatically!

There were no paper towels in the dispenser. Then I put my hands under the dispenser, and voilà, paper towels appeared!

Now, you may be thinking, Robert, that was no miracle—everything you mentioned above is action-motivated. But I beg to differ. If I had not moved; if I had stayed stagnant and not moved my feet or hands, I would still be in Tulsa. But I realized as soon as I started moving, things started happening.

When you take a step forward, doors open.

God is motion-activated! You are not waiting on God. He is waiting on you.

If you draw near to Him, He will draw near to you.

Recently I pulled lots of weeds in my garden. A few weeks later, my father, who has a green thumb, was at my house and commented, "Son, I thought you pulled these weeds a few weeks ago?!" I answered, "Yes, I did." He replied, "Then why are there still weeds in this garden?"

He continued, "You didn't pull the weeds in this garden. You just picked the leaves of the weeds! If you just pick the leaves in your garden, they will keep coming back again and again. In order for them not to come back again, you have to get down and pull that weed up from the root."

Often there can be weeds in the garden of your soul, and they hinder the beauty and the splendor of your life being displayed. Have you ever tried to get rid of something in your life, but it keeps coming back again and again? That's because you just "picked at the leaves." You need to let your heavenly Father reach down and pull up those weeds from the roots so healing can take place in your life.

God can speak to you through everything!

What would it be like for God to speak to you face to face? Can you imagine what it would have been like to have a conversation with Jesus? Not just to hear Him preach, but to sit down and talk to you!? Oprah and Dr. Phil have nothing on Jesus. The scriptures say He is a wonderful counselor!

One conversation with Jesus can change your life forever.

A Samaritan woman came to draw water, and Jesus told her, "Please give me a drink," since his disciples had gone off into town to buy food.

The Samaritan woman asked him, "How can you, a Jew, ask for a drink from me, a Samaritan woman?"

Jesus answered her, "If you knew the gift of GOD, and who it is who is saying to you, 'Please give me a drink,' you would have

been the one to ask him, and he would
have given you living water."

The woman told him, "Sir, you don't have a bucket, and the well
is deep. Where are you going to get this living water? You're not
greater than our ancestor Jacob, who gave us the well and drank
from it, along with his sons and his flocks, are you?"

Jesus answered her, "Everyone who drinks this water will be-
come thirsty again. But whoever drinks the water that I will give
him will never become thirsty again. The water that I will give him
will become a well of water for him, springing up to eternal life."

The woman said, "You must be a prophet!"
John 4:7-14, The Passion Translation

Before Jesus encountered the woman, he was with his disciples. He told them, "I NEED to go to Samaria." During that time
period, there was no association between Jews and Samaritans.
There was bad blood between the two sects. They avoided each
other at every turn. So it is noteworthy that the place where no
Jew went was the place where Jesus said, "I NEED to go there!"

The places where no one wants to go—that's where Jesus
wants to go. The people nobody wants to deal with—that's
who Jesus wants to talk to. Jesus is a Savior who wants to go to
the ostracized, the outcast, the unclean, and the unlovely.

When he gets to Samaria, he sits down on the well, and
waits to talk to one dysfunctional woman. Jesus was a man on
a mission—which he accomplished in just three years of ministry on earth. Yet He waited on one woman.

God is patient.

The woman arrives, sees Jesus, and proceeds to fill her water pot while Jesus is just sitting on the well. If I was the woman, and Jesus was sitting at the well, my reaction to seeing Jesus would NOT be just to fill up my water pot! I would be overwhelmed with excitement to see him!

But this woman did not react that way. She ignored Jesus.

Many people in the presence of Jesus are totally oblivious to His power to transform their life circumstance. This happens in church on a regular basis... "How long are they going to sing this song? When is he going to finish speaking?" All the while, Jesus is waiting right there to speak to you and transform your life.

Jesus engaged her in conversation, *"Excuse me, will you give me a drink?"*

Take off any lens you may have previously had—especially your religious paradigms. Look at this scripture from a totally different perspective. Put yourself in the shoes of this woman. She has had five husbands. And she is currently living with someone who is not her husband. (Sometimes the Bible reads like TMZ.) These were real people!

It cracks me up when someone says that God can't use them because of what they have done. I feel like asking them, "Have you read the Bible?!?!" The Bible is FULL of crazy stuff people have done. Murderers, cheats, adulterers, liars—yet God used them! The Holy Spirit edited the Bible to include lots of messed-up people. That means YOU are still a candidate for God to use.

If this woman had five husbands, and was living with a sixth, she was probably attractive. And she was used to men looking at her. In those days, typically women did not leave men, so more than likely, FIVE men left her. Five rejections. Five men telling her they were through with her.

She came to the well at noon. Only women came to the well. Not men. The well was a social gathering place. She arrived in the heat of the day, because she didn't want to see anyone. But there he was...a man...sitting at the well.

Put yourself in her shoes...she might have thought Jesus was looking for opportunities at the well, especially when his opening line to her was, *"Excuse me. Will you give me a drink?"*

She immediately responded, *"You are a Jew. I'm a Samaritan. We don't interact with each other."* And Jesus answered back, *"Girl, if you knew who I was..."* (That's my Robert Madu version.)

This woman illustrates something that will always impede us from receiving what God has for us—this woman allowed her perspective to become polluted by her past experiences. She thought the SEVENTH man she was meeting was just like the six she had encountered before.

In Biblical numerology seven is the number of completion and perfection. The other six men had depleted her. He came to her as the seventh man to complete her. He was there to give her exactly what her soul had been longing for. But she was about to miss this God moment because her perspective had become polluted by her past experiences.

If you are going to ever step into the FRESH and NEW... **you can never allow your perspective to become polluted by your past experiences.**

CHALLENGE OF LIFE

Do not drag your past experiences into your present circumstance. It's hard to avoid. Just being human makes us prejudiced. We draw conclusions based on our past experiences. But God is bigger than your past experiences. He wants to do something new and fresh in and through you.

You will make the fresh a mess if you pollute the present with your past experiences.

When I'm on a plane, I don't like to tell people I'm a preacher. I might say I'm in the oil business (anointing oil)—whatever to keep the conversation going. There are two extremes—one where they immediately clean up their language and the other where they say, "Oh, you're a PREACHER? Let me tell you about the CHUUURRCH....." Heads spin. They want to talk about the latest preacher in the news cycle. Their perspective has been polluted.

You can limit God with your perspective.

God is multi-dimensional. His power is far-reaching. Is it possible there is something God cannot do in your life because your perspective has become tainted? You don't need a new circumstance. You need a new perspective.

All God does is mighty works! We don't sing, "Our God is OK. Our God is alright. He can do some stuff; on some days He's average!" Dumbest praise and worship song EVER!

"Our God is Greater. Our God is Stronger. Our God is higher than any other!" (song written by Chris Tomlin)

Jesus was in Nazareth, his hometown. He went to reveal himself as the son of God. They couldn't see he was the son of God. All they saw was the son of Mary and Joseph. And because they couldn't see it, they couldn't receive.

He was unable to do any great miracle in Nazareth, except to heal a few sick people by laying his hands upon them.
Mark 6:5

When I discovered this truth, it took so much pressure off me as a preacher. I used to think the effectiveness of my preaching was all about what I said and how I presented the Word. But the perspective of the audience was the biggest factor in whether or not my preaching would leave a lasting impression and change lives.

How could two people be in the same exact service—one leave in tears, convicted and moved by the Holy Spirit; and the other one more interested in where to eat lunch?! It was their perspective! You cannot receive what you cannot perceive! What you see is what you get!

Open your eyes to see that God can do more abundantly than you can ask or think.

Expectancy—Expect And See!

The woman would not have been shocked Jesus spoke to her if she had known who He was. Jesus did not need her to give him water. Why did he ask her a question?

If Jesus asks you a question, the answer is never for him. The answer is for YOU!

He used the natural illustration of water to show her the dryness of her soul. She had been going from man to man, from situation to situation, trying to find something six men could never provide. She was trying to quench a spiritual thirst with something natural. That never works.

Thirst is not optional. Water is necessary.

"If I find in myself desires that nothing on this earth can satisfy, there is only one explanation. I was made for another world." C.S. Lewis

Something has crept into this generation—a spirit of discontentment. Social media has put steroids to discontentment. Discontentment is the offspring of a bad perspective.

When my wife and I have grudgingly climbed the stairs for the umpteenth time in the middle of the night to change a diaper...and yet I know a couple who would give ANYTHING to have a baby to care for...perspective. Fresh perspective.

Contentment does not come easily. Paul says in Philippians: *"I've learned whatever state I'm in...to be content."* He had to learn. He was writing from a jail cell. All the circumstances pointed to discontent. Paul had the "right" to be discontent. But God changed his perspective. Contentment is learned—it's a decision you must make.

There is a GLASS of WATER sitting on the table. You might doubt the existence of the water. You might question that there is a glass of water on that table. You might know some facts about water. You might even know some scriptures about water. But there is a difference between *knowing* about water, and *drinking* water. It quenches thirst!

It's the same with Living Water—Jesus. If you are thirsty, you can receive what He has to offer you—fresh and new and living water! But don't stop there. If you want all He has for you, DRINK the living water! It's there for you! Receive a fresh and new and vibrant way of living!

Change your perspective. He is the source of all things fresh and new!

✔ perspective Checkup

1. What do you run to trying to quench your thirst? Does it quench your thirst?

2. What do you reach for when discontentment comes? Does it bring contentment?

3. What steps can you take to avoid letting past circumstances impact your current perspective?

Conclusion

Throughout this book, I have done my best to push you to discover freshness in your daily life with God—to encounter ALL He has designed for you! And I hope that through these chapters, you have truly inspected your life, your attitude, your hope, your joys, and your perspective—and found that THERE CAN BE EVEN MORE for you in the days ahead!

As you open yourself to listening, meditating and obeying, may the freshness of the Holy Spirit envelop you and catapult you to every wonderful and delightful blessing He has prepared for you! May God bless you with FRESH!

—Jim Hennesy

Jim Hennesy

Jim Hennesy became the Senior Pastor of Trinity Church of the Assemblies of God, Cedar Hill, Texas, in November of 1994. Prior to that he served as Senior Pastor in St. Petersburg, Florida and Leeds, Alabama. He is a graduate of Central Bible College, Springfield, Missouri. With over 37 years of pastoral ministry, Jim leads Trinity Ministries into its finest hour as primary presenter of the preaching/teaching ministry and primary steward of Trinity's vision.

Jim focuses his ministry around the Presence and Testimony of Jesus (Substance of God), and strongly encourages the church to live in supernatural participation with the Holy Spirit.

Jim has also served as a visiting professor at North Central Bible College and Southwestern Assemblies of God University. He is a respected teacher and speaker at major gatherings of ministers around the world. Jim is author of the book, *No More Cotton Candy,* addressing the real substance of the Spirit-filled Christian life.

Jim, having a vision for the local church to impact the local community, helped found Transformation Vision Cedar Hill and serves on the steering committee. The organization is a coalition of business, education, government and churches committed to seeing God's principles enacted into the fiber and relationships of the community.

Jim leads a network of over 50 pastors across the nation and in Canada. He mentors, disciples, and meets with these pastors throughout the year. He also speaks to their congregations and conducts staff training.

Over the course of the last few years, Jim has traveled and spoken all over the world. Most recently, he spoke in Salvador, Brazil, eight times over three days to over 25,000 people. He leads workshops with church staff and elders when he visits these countries, as well.

Jim and Becky (married 41 years) have three children: Ross, a graduate of Texas Tech University and Temple University is currently the director of the Quaker Voluntary Service in Philadelphia. Ryan, a graduate of Southwestern University and Princeton Theological Seminary, and his wife, Julia, are on staff at a church in Baltimore. Katee, a graduate of Oral Roberts University, is currently serving on the executive staff at Trinity Church.